Fun WITH MY 5 SENSES

ACTIVITIES TO BUILD LEARNING READINESS

Sarah A. Williamson

Illustrations by Loretta Braren

WILLIAMSON PUBLISHING • CHARLOTTE, VERMONT 05445

Library of Congress
Cataloging-in-Publication Data
Williamson, Sarah, 1974-
    Fun with my 5 senses: activities to build learning
readiness / Sarah A. Williamson.
    p. cm. — (Little hands ; 10)
    Includes index.
    Summary: Presents a variety of activities
which build learning readiness for exploring and
understanding the five senses.
    ISBN 1-885593-19-8
    1. Early childhood education—Activity programs—
Juvenile literature. 2. Senses and sensation—Juvenile
literature. (1. Senses and sensation. 2. Youths'
writings.) I. Title. II. Series: Little Hands (Charlotte,
Vt.) ; 10.
LB1139.35A37W44 1998
372.21—dc21   97-50004
                                              CIP
                                              AC

Cover and interior design: Trezzo-Braren Studio
Illustrations: Loretta Braren
Printing: Capital City Press

Williamson Publishing Co.
P.O. Box 185
Charlotte, Vermont 05445
1-800-234-8791

Manufactured in the United States of America
10 9 8 7 6 5 4 3 2 1

Books by Sarah Williamson
Kids Cook! Fabulous Food for the Whole Family
by Sarah Williamson and Zachary Williamson

Little Hands® is a registered trademark of Williamson Publishing.

CONTENTS

To my Mom

Acknowledgements

A big thank you to Ken Braren and Loretta Trezzo-Braren for their inviting book design and vivid illustrations. As I wrote this book, I knew they would give life and humor to the experiences I envisioned children participating in.

And to my dear family and friends — especially my Dad, my brother Zachary Williamson, Dino Korten, Lynn Separk, Kerry Moyer, Poppit Sadtler, and Mike Lizotte — a very special thank you.

USING YOUR SENSES

Hey, Kids! It's A Bright, Noisy, Fun World

Did you know that you have some special tools with you all the time? That's right — whether you are riding in a car, playing in a sandbox, licking a dripping ice-cream cone, brushing your teeth — your special tools are always with you. Can you guess what these tools are?

There are actually five special tools called your five senses:

Sight that let's you see;

Hearing that brings you sounds;

Smell that brings you scents;

Taste that makes food yummy or yucky;

Touch that tells you about how something feels.

And the best thing is that you don't have to think about any of these senses or remember where you put them, because they are part of you. Yes, you have them with you right now!

You can put your five senses to work so you will observe more and more things around you. This will help you make better choices and have more fun every day. When we open up our senses to all the things around us, the world is filled with

- the colors of the rainbow and a field of dandelions

- the hum of insects and the rumble of passing trucks

- the smell of homemade bread or wet paint

- the taste of a juicy peach or a dill pickle

- the feel of your grandma's skin or a lamb's wool

There's lots of fun and good times packed in the pages that follow. You can enjoy these experiences and activities by yourself, with a friend, a sister or brother, or with a grown-up. You'll find things to do that use all of your senses from the top of your head to the tips of your toes. Along the way, you'll discover a lot of wonderful things about yourself and about the world around you.

So, have fun and don't forget to always use your five senses because you live in a bright, wonderful world — and you have all the tools to enjoy it!

For the Grown-Ups

I have written this book directly to the children in your lives because I know that they are ready, willing, and able to respond to my message. I wanted each of them to know I have confidence in their abilities to participate in these activities at whatever level they are comfortable.

The younger children will certainly need adult supervision, encouragement, and guidance in delving into these activities. There are no right and wrong ways to participate; no outcomes are more valuable than any others. The mere act of doing is in itself a big part of the learning and growing experience.

My hope is that the children who use this book will discover within themselves a great capacity for life's wonders. By enhancing their use of each of their senses, they will become more attuned to the nuances of every day and find beauty and meaning wherever they are at this moment and in their futures.

HEAR! HEAR!

Shhh! Listen. What do you hear?
Nothing?
Listen again, very carefully. Now what do you hear?
Wow! It sure is noisy out here!

TUMBLING RHYMES

It's fun to make rhymes (words that sound alike such as hike and like). It's even more fun to play a game using rhymes.

1 Find a place where you can do forward rolls without bumping into anything.

2 Play with two or more people; a group of four is perfect.

3 One person calls out a word. Then, another person stands up, calls out a rhyming word, and does a forward roll. Keep standing, rhyming, and rolling.

See who rolls the farthest. Then, begin again using a new word.

*Two words sound alike,
Now that's a rhyme.
It's easy to make —
Just take your time.*

CHICKEN!

In many poems, the words at the end of a line rhyme. But all poems certainly don't have to rhyme. Here's an example of a poem that doesn't rhyme:

The brown speckled bunny
*   scampered across the field*
As the stormy leaves swirled
*   to the rhythm of the wind.*

CHIMPANZEE!

MORE FUN!

♥ Instead of rhyming the end of the words, play Tumbling Sounds. Use the same rules, only this time match the beginning sounds of words like **ch**urch, **ch**ocolate, and **ch**impanzee.

♥ Play rhyming words during quiet time or in the car (without the somersaults, of course).

GOOD VIBRATIONS

Ta-dum, ta-dum,
   Ta-dum-dum-dum!
Vibrating sounds
   From the big drum.

You can't see sound, you can't taste sound, you can't smell sound. But guess what? You can actually feel sound!

HUMMMMMMM

1 Place your fingers lightly against the front of your throat. Now, hum loudly. What you feel is a vibration.

2 Place your hand on the floor near some speakers, on the back of a piano, or stand barefoot near some drums. Can you feel the vibrations of the sound waves?

❤ Want to see what sound waves look like? Drop a pebble in a basin of water. Notice the ripples? That's what sound waves would look like if you could see them.

EXPAND YOUR WORLD

Inside your ear is a thin membrane, or covering, that is something like the covering over a musical drum. This membrane vibrates when sound waves get trapped in your ear by your outer ears. Guess what they call this membrane? An eardrum!

HEAR! HEAR!

All ears are unique,
I bet you can see;
Your ears are different
Than the ears on me.

Ears may be pointy
    or they may be small;
Still perfect to hear
    Your mother's loud call.

The "ears" on the side of your head actually collect sound to send it to your inner ears. Ears come in all shapes and sizes.

FIDO HAS FLOPPY EARS

BILLY HAS CAULIFLOWER EARS

MARY HAS POINTED EARS

1 A funnel ear shape helps capture the sound waves. Cup your hands behind your ears and see if you can hear better.

2 Look in old magazines for pictures of animals. Which animals have the best ears for hearing?

3 Now make an ear collage. Cut out the animal ear pictures and glue on a piece of construction paper.

MY EAR COLLAGE

RABBIT

BAT

PIGGY

ELEPHANT

FOX

♥ Find a picture of a bat. Notice its big ears. How does the shape of the bat's ears help it to hear well?

♥ Make a headband and then create a set of ears shaped for good hearing.

EXPAND YOUR WORLD

Here are two ways to take care of your hearing. Never stick anything in your ears. And, don't listen to music turned up very loud. Can you think of any other ways to care for your hearing?

CLAPPING CLUES

Soft means cold,
Loud means hot,
When I'm close,
and when I'm not!

Listen closely to the clapping as it goes back and forth from loud to soft. It is the key to playing this game.

1 Play with two or more people. Someone hides an object; the player who is "It" hides his or her eyes.

2 Everyone begins clapping softly. "It" walks around the room. The closer "It" comes to the object, the louder the clapping becomes. The farther away, the softer the clapping. Play until the object is found and then play again.

CLAP
CLAP
CLAP
CLAP
CLAP
CLAP

EXPAND YOUR WORLD

The way Clapping Clues helped you is similar to the way bats avoid flying into people and buildings. Bats have excellent hearing and large ears. When they fly, they give off high-pitched squeaks that echo back to them, when something is in their path. The word for this — **echolocation** — means that an **echo** tells an object's **location**. Have you ever heard an echo?

♥ Teach each other some hand-clapping games such as "I am a Pretty Little Dutch Girl" or "Miss Mary Mac."

RIBBIT, RIBBIT

Here, there
Everywhere.
Out, in
The froggie spins.

Play this game with a partner to track down the croaking frog.

RIBBIT · RIBBIT

RIBBIT · RIBBIT

1 Sit on the floor and close your eyes.

2 Your partner (the frog) tiptoes barefoot quietly around you, sometimes up close, sometimes back a little ways, changing direction.

3 The frog stops and softly calls "ribbit." Now, you point to where you think the frog is standing. Were you right on target?

4 Change places so you can be the wandering frog.

RIBBIT

❤ Try cupping your hands around your ears. Does that make it easier to track the frog?

❤ Try covering one ear with your hand while you listen for the frog. Does that make it easier or more difficult to find it?

❤ Ask a grown-up to take you for a walk near a pond on a summer's night. Listen to the bullfrogs croaking. They are a very noisy chorus!

RIBBIT

STORYBOOK STEW

Listen carefully to what those who go before you say. Then, once it's your turn, twist the tale anyway you want. That's the fun of storybook stew — everyone can add whatever they want to the pot (oops, plot!) and then stir things up!

Here are some lead sentences to get you started:

"Once upon a time, there was a dragon who loved to eat carrots . . ."

"Zoe was having a perfectly miserable day . . ."

"Just as they brought out the cake, a baseball sailed through the open window . . ."

YUMMY YUMMY YUMMY CARROTS IN MY TUMMY!

♥ Develop your story backwards by telling the ending first.

♥ Here's a Storybook Stew Challenge! Listen carefully and then you have to begin your part of the story by repeating the last words of the person before you.

♥ Listen to *Jack and the Beanstalk*. A story where someone keeps trading one thing for another — connected like the links on a chain — is called a chain tale. Try making up a chain tale of your own.

CAN YOU HEAR MERMAIDS SINGING?

Hold the shell
Up to your ear
A quiet roar
For you to hear.

It is said that you can hear the ocean (or if you stretch your imagination, mermaids singing) by holding large, pink conch shells to your ear. Smaller conch-shaped shells work well, too. What is the shell saying to you?

1. Pick up a conch-shaped shell, make sure it is clean, and place it to your ear like a phone.

2. What do you hear? Describe the sound you hear.

3. Try it with different-shaped shells. Why do you think you only hear the sound with the conch-shaped shell?

MORE FUN!

♥ Collect some unusual, empty shells as you walk along the beach.

♥ Look in a shell field guide to identify the shells you collect.

♥ Paint some shells to give to friends as gifts.

NATURE'S SOUNDS

All day long we hear sounds all around us — people talking, dogs barking, cars honking, music playing. Give yourself a treat and listen for the quieter sounds of nature.

The sounds of nature
Call night and day,
So take a break
From your run-around play.

1 Sit outside and be as quiet as you can.

2 Let your ears adjust to the loud sounds around you. Now, listen carefully. Do you hear birds chirping? Leaves rustling? Bees buzzing? What other nature sounds do you hear?

PEEP
PEEP
CHIRP
RUSTLE
BUZZZZZ
PECK PECK PECK
WHOOOOO
SQUEAK

❤ Sketch a picture of all the things you hear making sounds. Is there a purring cat in your picture?

❤ Sit outside at twilight (just as the sun is setting). Listen to the night sounds. Do you hear crickets or frogs? Is that an owl? Compare the sounds of day and the sounds of night.

❤ Listen to the story *Too Much Noise!* by Ann McGovern.

❤ Create a nighttime theater! Shine a flashlight on a wall and using your hands to cast shadows, bring to life some animals of the night.

A FRIENDLY EAR

*If someone special
 is feeling blue,
And you are wondering
 what to do,
Sit and listen
 to what they say,
And you will help them
 have a good day!*

You can help someone turn a bad day into a better one. All that is needed sometimes is someone who is willing to listen — and that person could easily be you.

1 Spend some time with someone who seems extra quiet or sad.

2 Talk about something you have been doing for fun lately, and ask what they have been doing or thinking about.

3 Your friend may not want to talk, but don't be offended. Instead, just sit quietly together or tell a funny story about what happened to you in school.

EXPAND YOUR WORLD

If you find it difficult to listen without squirming and fiddling around, try this: Forget about yourself and your surroundings. Instead, look at the person who is talking. Then, ask a question about what you heard.

MORE FUN!

♥ Bring a boardgame to play with your friend — just the two of you.

♥ Look through some old magazines together. Talk about how the pictures make you feel.

♥ Ask older people to tell you about their school days. Then, listen carefully.

LittleHands

PHONEY PHONES

Ring, ring,
in my ear.
Is it the phone
that I hear?

Chat, chat,
with a friend.
Phone call fun
will never end!

Phoney phones aren't real telephones, of course, but you can have lots of fun with them anyway.

HERE'S WHAT YOU NEED

Cardboard tissue rolls (2)

String

HERE'S WHAT YOU DO

1 Ask a grown-up to make a small hole near the bottom of each tissue roll.

2 Thread your string through the hole and tie a knot.

3 Talk and listen through your phoney phones.

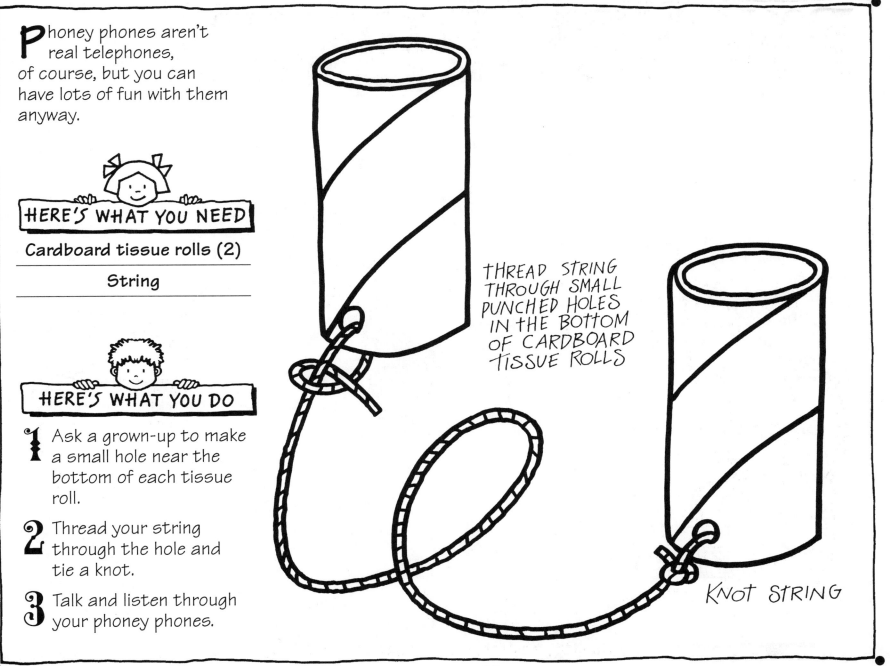

THREAD STRING THROUGH SMALL PUNCHED HOLES IN THE BOTTOM OF CARDBOARD TISSUE ROLLS

KNOT STRING

EXPAND YOUR WORLD

Are you learning to use the phone? Ask a grown-up to write the numbers you should call in an emergency in big numerals next to the phone. That way, in an emergency, you can pick up the receiver and dial the numbers yourself!

for Emergency dial 911

MORE FUN!

❤ Play Telephone Operator: Pass a message around a circle by whispering to the person next to you, who then whispers to the next person. Is the message at the end of the circle the same as the original message?

❤ Make a pretend phone dial. Practice "dialing" emergency numbers or your home phone number.

❤ Phones are fun. Ask a grown-up to help you call your grandparents or a friend on the phone. Practice listening and speaking into the receiver.

MUSIC FUN!

Music! Music! Music! It can make you feel like dancing, it can make you feel like singing, it can make you feel sad or happy, or happy and sad at the same time. Have fun with these musical listening games and get in the groove, 'cause now is the time to move!

MUSICAL ART

"Music without words," you say?
"Give me rock and roll to play."
Stop and listen to the sound,
Something special will be found.

HERE'S WHAT YOU NEED

Recording of Vivaldi's *The Four Seasons*

Drawing paper

Crayons or markers

We all know that paints and crayons are used to create beautiful pictures, but did you know that musical notes and rhythms can paint a picture, too?

Without using any colors, the composer (the person who writes the music) can create images of light and dark, happy or sad, winter or summer. Stop, listen, and feel the music, letting it sweep you away to a far-off land and time.

HERE'S WHAT YOU DO

1 Listen to Vivaldi's *The Four Seasons.*

2 Think about the pictures, or images, that the music brings to your mind. Can you imagine the different seasons? What else does the music remind you of?

3 Draw "listening" pictures. Add colors that reflect the mood the music puts you in. The composer was thinking of the four seasons of the year, but your drawings can show anything you want.

BY Me

♥ Write (or dictate) a story to complement your pictures.

♥ Ask a grown-up to play some jazz or some blues to draw to. How does different music make you feel? Does your jazz picture look different than your Vivaldi picture?

♥ Make a 3-D collage of your favorite season. Paste on pictures and three-dimensional objects that remind you of that season.

♥ Listen to the story *Frog and Toad All Year* by Arnold Lobel.

SOUND PATTERNS

High-pitch, low-pitch,
or somewhere in between;
Music's patterns
can actually be seen.

Some music is played in a very high pitch; other music is low-pitched; most music is a pleasing combination of both highs and lows. Here's a way to draw what you hear.

1 Sit down with a marker and paper. Put on a piece of classical music (a string quartet is good for this activity).

2 Listen for a while and then use dots to show the sound patterns. Place a dot at the top of the page for a high note and a dot near the bottom for a low note.

3 Then connect the dots for a high-low sound pattern.

EXPAND YOUR WORLD

Sometimes, when listening to music, you will hear very short notes like a quick tap or the plucking of a string. This is called **staccato**. If you like to dance, staccato music makes you feel like dancing on your tippy toes.

MORE FUN!

♥ Listen again to the music. This time mark dots for quick notes and dashes for notes that are held for a long time. Then, tap out the pattern on the floor.

♥ Now listen for loud and soft sounds. Jump up like a frog for loud sounds; curl up like a kitten for soft sounds.

♥ Listen to the voices in your household. Do the voices all sound the same? Are there differences between the men's and women's voices?

FREEZE DANCE

Dance around,
This game is fun.
Jump and sway
And even run.

Listen well
While in the groove,
When the music's off,
You cannot move.

Freeze Dance is lots of fun, especially if you listen to different kinds of music: stretch with some blues, jitter with rock, sway with jazz, and march with some parade beats. Just remember to STOP when the music stops.

1. The leader or "judge" plays the music and decides who is moving when the music stops. The music is played long enough so the players can get into it.

2. Everyone else listens carefully, and swings, sways, and rocks according to how the music makes them feel.

3. When the music stops, the dancers freeze. No moving — not even your little finger — until the music starts again. Last one dancing becomes the judge when you all play again.

Hint: Once you are out, play on your own off to the side until the next round. Good practice and good fun!

MORE FUN!

♥ The judge can try to make the players laugh — make funny faces, tell funny jokes. If the players laugh, they are out.

♥ Take the Freeze Dance Challenge: Play with a partner. Pairs must be touching when the music stops.

♥ All players freeze in the position the judge calls out. "Everyone on one foot!"

DRINKING GLASS BAND

*U*se a glass
Tap out the beat,
Fill it up,
It's pretty neat.

Then grab a pan
To make a drum,
A marching band
Is so much fun!

Want to make some music? All you need are some drinking glasses and a little water — and you'll be ready to rock and roll!

HERE'S WHAT YOU NEED

Water glasses (3)

Water

Spoon

HERE'S WHAT YOU DO

1. Fill glasses with water to three different levels.

2. Arrange glasses in a row from lowest water level to highest.

3. Gently tap the rim of the glass with the spoon.

4. What do you notice about the sound and the water level? That's right, the more water the higher the sound.

EXPAND YOUR WORLD

Marching music is so much fun. You can hardly sit still when it is playing. Play some of John Philip Sousa's marches (ask in a library for a recording), make some parade hats out of newspaper, gather up your homemade instruments so you can play along, and march, march, march.

MORE FUN!

♥ Use 5 glasses filled from low to high. Hum "Three Blind Mice" and then tap it out on your water glass.

♥ Add instruments to your band. Use an old pot and wooden spoon as a drum, dried beans in paper bags for maracas, shake some bells, or tap two pieces of wood together for a wonderful clackety-clack sound.

♥ Learn how to play the empty bottle horn. Blow gently *across* (not into) the top of an empty bottle to make a sound.

♥ Take turns with your friends being the conductor.

RED-HOT POTATO

Red-hot potato
in your hand,
Passed to the music
of the band.

Don't forget to pay attention to the music, as you watch the potato go 'round and 'round. Think about what a hot potato would feel like in your hands to help you pass it quickly. You'll laugh and laugh as everyone scrambles to get rid of it.

1 One person is Music Maker, facing away from the players. Everyone else sits in a circle.

2 When the music starts, pass the potato (an object like a tennis ball or bean bag) around the circle. Make sure to pass it quickly — that potato is hot!

3 When Music Maker stops the music, the person holding the potato becomes the new Music Maker.

MORE FUN!

♥ Play hot potato standing in a circle. Bounce a ball to the player next to you instead of passing it.

♥ Count together out loud how many times the potato is passed before the music stops.

♥ Bake a potato with a grown-up. Top it with cheese, veggies, or salsa for a yummy treat.

ROUND & ROUND WE GO

One group starts,
To sing its part.
Then on cue,
It comes to you.

Singing in a round involves two kinds of listening. First you listen to the others sing, so that you can hear your cue (when you start singing). Then, you listen to yourself and try to block out everything else.

1 Break into three groups.

2 Select a very simple song like "Row, Row, Row Your Boat."

3 Sing the song through a couple of times together (called singing in **unison**), for practice.

4 Then, the first group begins. The second group begins at the word "stream," with the third joining in when the second group says stream.

5 Each group sings the whole song three times. If it gets all confused, try again. Singing in rounds is lots of fun!

ROW, ROW, ROW YOUR BOAT GENTLY DOWN THE STREAM...

ROW, ROW, ROW YOUR BOAT GENTLY DOWN THE STREAM MERRILY, MERRILY, MERRILY, MERRILY...

ROW, ROW, ROW YOUR BOAT GENTLY DOWN THE STREAM MERRILY, MERRILY, MERRILY, MERRILY LIFE IS BUT A DREAM!

MORE FUN!

♥ Do a round singing "Twinkle, Twinkle Little Star" or "Frere Jacques."

♥ When people sing together it is called a **chorus** or **choral music**. For a real treat, listen to The Mormon Tabernacle Choir or The Boys Choir of Harlem. What a wonderful sound!

Feel shy about singing?
Sing in a chorus with
lots of other people or
sing in the shower all by
yourself. Don't know the
words? Make them up
or sing nonsense words.
Whatever you do, sing,
sing, sing!

THE NOSE KNOWS

Sometimes we forget about our sense of smell — unless something smells really bad like a rotten egg or really good like an apple pie! Our noses can do a lot more, as you will see — oops — smell here!

SNIFFLES & SNEEZES

Sniffles and sneezes
Bring more than wheezes,
Even peppermint sticks
Have no taste when I'm sick.

All stuffed up from a cold? Besides a red and runny nose, nothing tastes very good either. You may be surprised to learn why.

1 Ask a grown-up to prepare some taste treats such as a slice of orange, some cinnamon toast, and a peppermint candy.

2 Put one of the treats in your mouth. Mmm-good!

3 Now, hold your nose tightly and try a treat. How does it taste? Try again without holding your nose. How does it taste now?

EXPAND YOUR WORLD

A lot of our sense of taste is really our sense of smell. Isn't that a surprise? No wonder a stuffy nose makes food seem tasteless. We can't smell it!

TISSUES

MORE FUN!

♥ Ask a friend to close eyes, nose pinched closed, mouth opened wide. Place a small piece of orange in his or her mouth. Can your friend guess what kind of food it is?

♥ Next time you have to take a bad-tasting medicine, don't fret. Just hold your nose and guess what? That's right — you won't be able to taste it!

♥ Make up a story about a nose that couldn't smell.

TASTES GREAT!

Sweet or sour,
Spicy, bland,
Varied tastes
Make food grand!

Most everyone has a favorite food. You may also have a favorite flavor like chocolate or strawberry. How many different foods can you name that have your favorite flavor? Hmm, there's strawberry ice cream, strawberry jam, strawberry yogurt . . .

Taste each of the following foods and say whether it is **sweet, sour, spicy, bland** (without any noticeable taste), or **salty**.

Pickle

Chocolate chip

Hard-boiled egg

Salsa

Lemon

Cracker

Peppermint candy

SWEET
SOUR
SPICY
BLAND

❤ Describe to a friend how your favorite food tastes.

❤ Play Taste Tester. Name a food (peach) and ask a partner to name its taste (sweet). Do you agree on all the tastes? Then, play in reverse: Name a taste and your partner names a food with that taste.

❤ Why do you think in some places of the world people eat a lot of one kind of food and in other places people eat a lot of a different food?

❤ Plan a picnic menu with four different tastes in it. Then, spread a blanket and enjoy your picnic — indoors or out!

FLOWER POWER

Springtime flowers
Come with showers
Blossoms smell sweet
Oh, what a treat!

Ah, the smells of spring! We open our windows to "air out" the house — which really means to let the stale winter air out and the sweet-smelling spring air inside. But all flowers don't smell the same. Let your nose show you.

1 Take your nose outdoors into the flower garden, to a park, or to a flower shop.

2 Now choose a flower. Lean over and take a deep breath, breathing in the lovely perfume.

3 Here are some flowers to smell: roses, hyacinths, lilacs, allium, stock, gardenias, marigolds. What words would you choose to describe the smell of each kind of flower?

EXPAND YOUR WORLD

There are lots of different words to use when you want to say "That has a good (or bad) smell." We talk about food's **aroma**, flowers' **fragrance**, body **odor**, and perfume's **scent**.

MORE FUN!

♥ Some flowers don't really have much of a scent — at least not that we humans can smell. Can you find any in the garden that don't seem to smell?

♥ William Shakespeare, a famous British author who lived over 450 years ago, wrote "A rose by any name would smell as sweet." Now that you have smelled lots of flowers, what do you think he meant?

♥ If you are allowed to pick some flowers (please ask permission), take just a few, snip the stems short, wrap in wet paper towel and then in foil, attach a safety pin, and give to someone for a Flower Power Corsage.

A SNIFFING HOUSE TOUR

Some places at home just have familiar smells — the garage smells like gasoline, the kitchen smells like good food (well, most of the time!), and maybe the family room smells like a wood fire in the fireplace. Take time to notice the sweet and sour smells around your house.

Most people
   notice a room
      from its shape and size.
But if you
   notice its smell,
      it's quite a surprise!

1 Walk into the kitchen in late afternoon. Can you tell what is for dinner without looking or asking? Take a "nose knows" guess.

2 Step into the family room or living room. Can you smell who was there — Grandma's perfume, your mom's favorite soap, your wet dog curled up in the corner?

3 Visit a bedroom. Are those smelly sneakers that you're sniffing? An old apple core rotting under your bed? Your big brother's workout clothes? (Uh-oh, not all smells are sweet smells!)

MY SNIFFING TOUR

BEST SMELLS	WORST SMELLS
MOM'S PIE	SNEAKERS
FLOWERS	GARBAGE
DINNER	ROVER

MORE FUN!

♥ Name the three best smells you found in your Sniffing Tour and the three worst smells.

♥ Use as many different words as you can to describe the smells in a baby's room.

♥ Be a kitchen smell detective: Did someone have toast for breakfast? Burn the cookies in the oven? Make popcorn? Forget to take out the garbage? Cook fish for dinner?

SAFETY SMELLS

Your sense of smell
Is lots of fun;
It also tells
If you should run.

GOOD SMELL?

BAD SMELL?

Knowing noses do lots more than bring good and bad smells into our lives and help us taste our food. Your well-trained nose can actually give you messages that could save your life or keep you healthy.

Talk about these things with a grown-up:

1. You smell smoke in your house. What does it mean? What should you do?

2. You smell natural gas in your house or outdoors. What does it mean? What should you do?

3. You smell wet paint. What should you do?

4. You smell glue and other art supplies while you are doing arts and crafts. What should you do?

5. You hear a smoke alarm or carbon monoxide alarm. What should you do?

SMOKE?

GAS?

SMOKE ALARM?

GLUE?

WET PAINT?

❤ Play a game of Safety Smells: One person describes a time, a place, and a smell. The other person tells where to go and what to do.

❤ Talk about ways that your sense of sight, hearing, touching, and smelling protects you.

❤ Learn the emergency phone number and post it by every phone in the house. Then ask a grown-up to help you practice it.

❤ Find an emergency exit from your bedroom. Make a plan to leave your house safely in case you cannot exit through the front door.

❤ Make exit signs to place over all of the main exits in your house. Ask a grown-up to put child safety stickers in your bedroom window.

❤ Visit the fire station.

Knowing how to **stop**, **drop**, and **roll** in case you ever catch on fire is very important. It is easy to do, so let's practice. Should you ever catch fire anywhere on your body or your clothes:

Stop: Don't run. Stop where you are.

Drop: Drop to the ground or floor, pulling your arms in toward your body.

Roll: Roll your body over and over, as if you were rolling down a hill. This will put out the flames.

   And remember: Never, ever play with matches.

SUMMER SCENT WALK

The smells of summer
Sure do abound,
Discoveries await,
To be found.

Isn't summer fun? Spin around with your arms stretched out and breathe in and out — very s-l-o-w-l-y! Mmm, Mmm — summer smells good, too!

Take a walk with a grown-up and soak up the smells of summer. Search out new scents with your new smelling smarts! Here are some things to get you started:

Smell the freshly mowed lawn,

the tomato plants in the garden,

fresh soil in your hands,

the rose bushes and marigolds,

the neighbor's barbecue,

a walk through the woods,

a rainy summer day,

the seashore,

suntan lotion.

MORE FUN!

♥ What are some new smells you noticed during your walk?

♥ Think of the other seasons and talk about what they smell like.

♥ Divide a paper into four sections: Draw a picture of the smells of each season.

♥ Make a plan to take the same walk at another time of year to see if the smells are different in the same places.

ANIMAL SCENTS

My puppy walks
    with her nose to the ground,
She seems to know
    something good's to be found.

Sniff, sniff. Paw, paw. Dogs are always searching with their noses for a hidden treasure — the kind they can eat! Many animals depend on their sense of smell to help them find food.

1 Watch a dog let loose in a yard. What do you notice about how it uses its nose? How do you suppose a dog finds a bone that it hides outdoors?

2 Watch some squirrels in the fall. They're busy hiding their nuts for winter food. How will they be able to find the nuts?

BONY

Many people think squirrels remember where they bury their nuts. Actually, they have a very good sense of smell, and they can locate nuts buried under many inches of snow by smelling them.

MORE FUN!

♥ Let your dog smell a treat. Then hide it out of sight, like behind a chair. Can the dog find it? Hide another treat.

♥ Do you think cats have a sense of smell, too? Try the same experiment, this time hiding a cat treat in an unusual place. Does your cat find it?

♥ Hide another treat. This time count how long it takes your pet to find it. Count seconds, saying "One elephant, two elephants, three. . ."

WINDOW-BOX HERB GARDEN

Herbs add lots of flavor to foods, and you already know why. That's right, because they have such strong scents. Plant a window-box herb garden for year-round scent-sations.

They smell so sweet
And taste so neat.
They grow so well
Herbs sure are swell!

HERE'S WHAT YOU NEED

Small plant pots

Potting soil

Herb seedlings (mint, thyme, basil, oregano)

Pie tins or drip catchers

HERE'S WHAT YOU DO

1 Cover bottom of pots with small pebbles; then fill to 3/4 with potting soil.

2 Gently place a seedling in each pot, spreading out the roots. Then cover with more soil and pat down.

3 Place on drip catchers; water, and place in a sunny window.

4 Keep moist but not soaked. Snip off herbs, as needed.

PUT SMALL PEBBLES ON BOTTOM OF POT

FILL POT 3/4 FULL WITH SOIL

PLACE SEEDLING IN POT, SPREAD ROOTS

COVER ROOTS WITH MORE SOIL, PAT SOIL DOWN

PUT POT IN DRIP CATCHER, KEEP MOIST, AND CLIP HERBS AS NEEDED

MORE FUN!

❤ Crumple fresh herbs — one at a time — in your hand. Then smell them.

❤ Herbal taste treats: Use your freshly snipped herbs in iced tea (mint), spaghetti sauce (oregano, basil), salads (basil). Experiment with other foods.

❤ Take an herbal bath: Snip some fresh herbs like thyme, basil, lemon balm, or lavender and place on some cheese-cloth. Tie with a ribbon and add to the tub for a kid-soothing bath.

I SEE IT NOW!

Most of us are fortunate to have two eyes with which to see; some of us even get to wear eyeglasses to help us see better. But your eyes can do more. They can be a window on the world — if you take the time to look closely and carefully — and if you use your imagination, too!

WIDE-EYED NATURE WALK

Open your eyes
Wide as can be,
Look with your heart
What do you see?

Look with your heart? Yes, that's right. No sense going on a nature walk without opening your eyes wide, thinking about what you see all around you, and bringing the spirit of fun and curiosity (that's the heart part) along on your walk, too. Here we go!

Go on a walk with at least one grown-up, and maybe a couple of friends, too. The idea is to see things that you usually don't notice. Point out things to your friends along the way.

Here are some things to look for depending on the time and place:

a bird's nest in a tree

a woodpecker's fresh hole in a tree

nut shells on the ground

buds just about to open on bushes

the first autumn leaves

moss growing on a tree or rock

earthworms hiding under a log

a snake sunning on a rock

milkweed pods opening up

furry caterpillars on a path

a spider web in the tall grass

a wasp's nest way up in a tree

pine needles on the forest floor

a puffball mushroom in the woods

a cottontail scampering away

deer tracks in the snow.

EXPAND YOUR WORLD

Take a walk on Earth Day (April 22), bring along a garbage bag, and collect anything that nature didn't intend to have you see (bottles, cans, papers, and other trash).

MORE FUN!

♥ What did you see that was a big surprise to you? What didn't you see that you were hoping to see?

♥ Take a nature walk at different times of year to see how nature changes.

♥ Go on a single subject search, such as a caterpillar search. Then count how many caterpillars you see on your walk.

♥ Look closely at three things you see on your walk, such as butterflies, a piece of bark, and a sparkling rock. After your walk, make up a story about these three things. Ask a grown-up to write down your story, leaving room for you to draw the pictures.

FIND THAT PAINTING!

Museums are too boring,
    You might say.
So, look at them
    In a whole new way.
Buy a postcard,
    Search high and low,
The real painting
    You'll soon get to know.

A museum can be a lot of fun, especially if you are on a mission. This is a game between you and the paintings on the wall. Look closely and you will be surprised by all you can see!

1 Visit the museum's gift shop and buy one postcard of a painting that is in the museum.

2 Look closely at your postcard. Does the painting tell a story?

3 Now, walk quietly through the museum; be on the lookout for the painting on your postcard.

4 Yeah, you found it! Do you see things in the real painting that you didn't notice on the postcard?

MUSEUM POSTCARD

TO:

EXPAND YOUR WORLD

Look in the museum for other paintings by the same artist. Does the artist use similar colors, paint the same subject, or use the same kinds of paint? These features are called the artist's **style**.

MORE FUN!

❤ Try out some water-colors, tempera paint, and finger paint. How do they look different?

❤ Visit the library to look for books about the artist on your postcard.

❤ Paint your own painting in a way you think the artist might paint it. Or, paint something special in your very own style!

❤ Describe to a friend what you liked and didn't like about the artist's painting. Show your friend the postcard.

THE BETTER TO SEE YOU WITH

Protect your eyes —
From sun too bright
And things too sharp —
To have good sight.

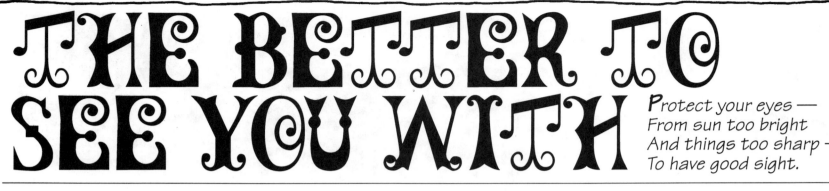

Look in a mirror to see what color eyes you have. Knowing your eyes' color is just for fun; knowing how to take care of your eyes is serious business!

1 Hold your finger in front of your face.

2 Now, without moving your head, move your finger slowly to one side of your face and then slowly to the other side. Can you see it or does it move out of view?

3 Here are three things you can do to protect your eyes. Can you think of any more?

Don't look directly at the sun or other bright lights.

Keep sharp objects like pencils and knitting needles away from your eyes.

Don't rub your eyes with dirty hands.

DON'T LOOK DIRECTLY AT THE SUN

KEEP SHARP OBJECTS AWAY FROM EYES

DON'T RUB EYES WITH DIRTY HANDS

MORE FUN!

❤ Draw some pictures to help you remember how to take care of your eyes.

❤ Act out the story of *Little Red Riding Hood*.

EXPAND YOUR WORLD

Eyeglasses are very special. They help people to see. If you wear glasses, you get to pick out the color frames that you like best. Count how many pairs of eyeglasses you see today. Lots and lots, I bet!

CLOUD CHARACTERS

Each cloud looks different,
As you know,
Way up above,
Soft as the snow.

Lie on your back
Face to the sky,
Oh, yes, they're different,
As you and I.

Spend a lazy afternoon lying on your back, looking at the clouds. Just relax, and let your imagination go. In no time, animal shapes will take flight, as fanciful objects float by.

1 Look up at the clouds. What **shapes** do the clouds make? What do these shapes remind you of?

2 What **colors** are the clouds and the sky?

3 Share your cloud-gazing with a friend. Compare what you see in the clouds with what your friend sees.

EXPAND YOUR WORLD

If the weather person says it is going to be "partly cloudy" outside, it means that the sky will be grey with clouds, but that the sun will peek through every now and then. Partly cloudy days are good for working in the garden and playing at the playground.

MY CLOUD BOAT

♥ Make up a silly story about the images you see. Hmm, let's see: Do you happen to see a flying sheep and an enormous flower?

♥ Talk about how you feel on a day with blue sky and white fluffy clouds. How do you feel on a cloudy day with heavy grey clouds and no sunshine?

♥ Listen to the book *Cloud Over Clarence* by Marc Brown.

♥ Design some cloud shapes, using cotton balls, glue, and construction paper.

HOW MANY?

*How many objects
Do you see?
A penny, a pencil,
One, two, or three?*

*Is one missing?
Oh, that's swell!
If you know,
Will you tell?*

If you look carefully, and think about what you see, you'll begin to notice the changes around you.

1 Place three to five different, small objects on the floor.

2 Ask your partner to study the objects and then turn around.

3 Remove one object.

4 Ask your partner to look and guess which object was removed. Give some hints, such as "It was next to the stone." Next time you turn around.

MORE FUN!

♥ Make it more difficult. Remove an object and then rearrange the ones that are left, or, remove two objects at a time.

♥ Play with seven objects to really get stumped.

♥ Bake different-shaped cookies using cookie cutters. Play the game using the cookies. The correct answer wins a cookie. Bake lots of extra cookies so everyone gets a treat!

FALL LEAF FESTIVAL

Fall is a season
Of color and zest,
Why not celebrate
With your own Fall Fest!

Celebrate fall! Look at the beautiful leaves and breathe in the crisp air. Then make a banner aglow with the shapes and colors of fall.

HERE'S WHAT YOU NEED

Paper bag, medium-size

Piece of butcher paper

Glue

Tempera paint, autumn colors

1 When autumn leaves are everywhere, take a walk, bring along a bag, and open your eyes wide.

2 What do you see? Leaves, leaves, leaves. Now look more closely. What do you see? **Pointed** leaves, **rounded** leaves. **Big** leaves, **little** leaves. **Red** leaves, **yellow** leaves.

3 Collect your favorite leaves in your bag.

4 Now, spread some butcher paper on the floor, ask a grown-up to help you write "Hooray for Fall" in big letters, and paint the letters in bright fall colors with tempera paint.

5 Glue your leaves around the border of your banner and hang.

MORE FUN!

♥ Go apple picking, and then bake a fresh apple pie (with the help of a grown-up).

♥ Warm some cider with a grown-up's help. Then, add a little cinnamon for a real fall treat.

♥ Volunteer to help rake the leaves in your yard. Then, jump into the piles!

STILL LIFE

Drawing pictures of fruit and bread,
It's not too hard, just use your head.
Such good models — they won't wiggle,
And tickles don't make them giggle.

Painting a still-life picture of an apple and banana, or a baseball bat and a catcher's mitt will open your eyes to the smallest details of colors and shapes.

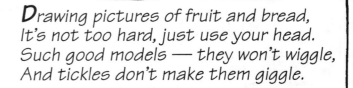

HERE'S WHAT YOU NEED

Poster board or painting paper

Markers

2 objects to paint

HERE'S WHAT YOU DO

1 Spread some newspaper where you are drawing.

2 Arrange the objects any way that you want.

3 Using your markers, draw what you see. Is the apple perfectly round? Does the bat have some scratches?

♥ Experiment with watercolors, chalk, or colored pencils.

♥ Why do you think they call this kind of painting "still life"?

♥ Draw some fruit. Once you have finished your drawing, make a still-life fruit salad!

COLOR TAG

Red, orange,
White, green,
Shout the color
That you mean.

Purple, pink,
Black, blue.
Tag it or —
Out goes YOU!

Colors are all around **C**us. Here's a way to have fun playing tag and to sharpen your color skills, too!

1 Everyone stands up.

2 One person shouts out a color like, "Red!"

3 Everyone runs to tag something that is red. Only one person can tag any one object.

4 Then, someone else calls out another color. Keep playing until you've color-coded the whole space you are in.

RED

BLUE

💙 Play sitting down: Call out a color, and then go around in a circle, each person naming an object that color.

💙 Talk about things that change color like tomatoes on the vine.

💙 Take the color challenge! This time call out an object (like a banana), and say its usual color (yellow).

SHADES OF COLOR

Blue for a baby,
Blue as the sky,
Here is the shade,
That matches my eyes!

Note: This activity works best with a jumbo pack of Crayola™ Crayons.

I don't know if anyone has ever counted all the different shades of blue. Robin's-egg blue, sky blue, baby blue, bright blue, navy blue, turquoise blue, azure blue — wow! What do all these names mean? They are all different shades, or variations, of the color blue.

1 Think about the basic colors you know: red, blue, green, yellow.

2 Spill all of the crayons onto the floor in front of you. Then sort them into piles: a red shades pile, a blue shades pile, a green shades pile, and a yellow shades pile. (There will be other colors left over.)

3 Count how many crayons are in each pile.

4 Test some of the colors on a piece of paper. Then, pick out your favorite shade of each color.

There are lots of uses for the word shade. You draw with different **shades of color.** You **close the shades** when you want to keep the sun out of a room. You **sit in the shade** when you want to get out of the hot sun. And, you **wear shades** when you want to keep the sun out of your eyes (and look cool, too).

MORE FUN!

💙 Take the shady challenge. Look at all of the red crayons and put them in line starting with the lightest red (probably a light pink) to the darkest red (probably a dark red called maroon). Try it with other colors.

💙 Do a light/dark scratch painting. Color a piece of paper all over in light colors. Press the crayons down hard. Now, cover over the crayons with a dark blue, dark green, or black crayon. Take a toothpick and scratch a design through the top color to the bottom colors.

💙 Look in your closet and find three things that are different shades of the same color.

STAINED-GLASS WINDOWS

Color, color, and more color! That's what make stained-glass windows so beautiful.

The light shines through,
The colors flow,
Oh, beautiful windows
You're all aglow.

HERE'S WHAT YOU NEED

Colored cellophane

Construction paper

Child safety scissors

Glue

String

HERE'S WHAT YOU DO

1 Fold two pieces of construction paper in half. Cutting through both pieces of paper at once, cut out a square shape along the fold, leaving a wide, uncut border. You now have two identical frames.

2 Cut a piece of colored cellophane to fit in your frame. Glue the edges of the cellophane to the edges of one piece of your frame.

3 Now glue the other half of the frame on top of the cellophane.

4 Hang your frame by a string in front of a sunny window. What do you see when the light shines through?

FOLD 2 PIECES OF PAPER TOGETHER & CUT OUT CENTER

CUT CELLOPHANE

GLUE OTHER HALF ON TOP

MORE FUN!

❤ Make more stained-glass windows in different shapes and in different colors. Hang them near one another.

❤ Visit a place where you can see some stained-glass windows.

A CLOSER LOOK

*S*ometimes taking a closer look means taking the time to notice all the details such as the white "boots" on a grey cat's paws or the different colors in a flower garden. Othertimes, you might want the help of a pocket magnifying glass to take an even closer look.

BE A JITTERBUG

Stop to take a look around,
    Looking up from the ground
Scrunch way down small as can be,
    A bug's world, you to see!

Everyone likes to play "pretend," so why not pretend that you are a very small bug? Pick any bug you want — a busy ant, a delicate daddy longlegs, a bold beetle, or a creeping caterpillar. Crawl around to see the world from a bug's point of view.

1 Get down on your hands and knees or lie flat on your tummy outside in your yard.

2 Look up, down, all around. Notice how different everything looks from the ground.

3 Now look even more closely at the ground. Here are some things to look for: individual blades of grass, other bugs crawling on the ground, dew drops or tiny webs on the grass, earthworms.

MORE FUN!

♥ Draw a picture of the ground from your bug's viewpoint.

♥ Go indoors and crawl bug-style through each room in your house. What do you see that you usually miss when you are standing up?

♥ Imagine you are a giant. How would everything look if you towered above the ground? Would you rather be a tiny bug on the ground or a towering giant?

DETECTIVE FOR A DAY

A detective's job is hard to do,
Snooping around to find a clue.
A magnifier helps to spy,
What isn't seen with the naked eye.

For a detective, looking carefully is very important. How else will you be able to see finger smudges and footprints?

1 Look around your house or classroom. Do you notice anything unusual?

2 Now go back and look at objects using a magnifying glass. What does the magnifying glass tell you about texture? Do you see any smudges on tables?

3 Talk about the times when a magnifying glass helps you in your detective work and when it doesn't.

EXPAND YOUR WORLD

Detectives look for finger-prints, because everyone in the whole wide world has different fingerprints. Take a trip to your local police station and get a copy of your fingerprints made.

❤ Once you have explored your house, take your magnifying glass outside to inspect your backyard.

❤ Detectives sometimes look for footprints as clues to solve a mystery. Based on the animal tracks outdoors, what kind of animals do you suppose were there?

❤ Make your own tracks. Spray the bottom of your bare feet with water. Then, walk on the sidewalk.

WHO WAS HERE?

Knitting needles,
Sweet perfume,

Cup of tea,
That's the key.

Who was here?
It's so clear —

Auntie Lark
Left her mark!

Look in a room for clues that tell you who was there and what they were doing.

Here are some things to look for:

Newspapers, books, checkers, chess, playing cards, eyeglasses, box of cookies, crumpled pillows, favorite sweater, slippers.

Then, connect what you observe with the people you know.

DAD

SIS

♥ Give clues to someone and then let them guess who you are describing.

♥ Draw a picture of a room just the way it would look **after** a person left it.

♥ What would a person see in a room that you just left?

WATER WORLD

Upon first glance,
The water is clear,
But look again,
As creatures appear.

Many creatures call a pond home. Because you are looking closely now, you will see so much more than ever before.

HERE'S WHAT YOU NEED

Grown-up

Bucket

Pocket magnifying glass

Paper and colored pencils

HERE'S WHAT YOU DO

1 Have a grown-up take you to a pond.

2 Carefully collect some pond water in your bucket.

3 Examine it closely, first by looking at it with your unaided eyes, and then with the aid of your magnifying glass.

Look for: floating grasses and bits of soil, yellow pollen, algae (green pond scum), tadpoles, tadpole eggs in a slimy jelly, turtles, fish, water bugs, cattails, reeds.

EXPAND YOUR WORLD

Using a magnifying glass certainly does make things appear larger. If you want to see even smaller things enlarged, use a microscope. Collect some pond water in a small container. Look at it on a slide under a microscope at home or in school. What squirming things do you see?

MORE FUN!

♥ No pond? Try a big puddle after a heavy rain.

♥ Pack a picnic to bring on your pond visit.

♥ A pond is a good place to listen, too. What kinds of sounds do you hear?

♥ Bring binoculars and look for birds like ducks or herons.

♥ Look for animal footprints and notice where they are going.

ZOO VISIT

So many animals around,
The zoo is the best place to visit in town.
Which animal do you like best?
I think the giraffe stands above all the rest.

The zoo is a great place to practice your looking skills. After all, there are so many different kinds of animals to see.

1 While walking through the zoo, use your looking skills to notice different animals' physical (body) characteristics. Two legs or four? Feathers or fur? Land or water? Trees or ground?

2 Then, stand in front of one kind of animal — maybe at the monkey house, the bear den, or the bird aviary. Use your looking skills again, picking out the differences that you see even in one kind of animal. Bigger or smaller? Dark colored or light colored? Quick or slow moving? Clumsy or graceful? Friendly or distant? Even animals that supposedly are the same have lots of differences when you look closely.

EXPAND YOUR WORLD

Do you have a favorite animal? It's fun to collect pictures and poems, stories and playthings that feature a favorite animal. Maybe yours will be an elephant, frog, or ostrich. Whatever, learn all you can about it, become a *Favorite Animal Expert* and start a *Favorite Animal Collection.*

❤ Before going to the zoo, look at pictures of one special kind of animal. Then, help the other kids by pointing out details to notice.

❤ Everyone in your family or in your classroom is a kind of animal — a human being. What things are the same about people? What things are different?

❤ No zoo nearby? Visit a local farm, pet store, aquarium, or museum of natural history.

BEAUTIFUL BIRDS

Tweet, tweet,
    what's that up in the tree?

A little bird
    for all to see.

Is it hungry?
    It needs a treat-

Something special
    for it to eat.

Describing birds is easy, you might say: feathers, wings, beaks, spindly little legs. Look again and tell what you see — wow! Birds come in all shapes, sizes, colors, and even with spots and stripes, too!

1 Set up a bird feeder where you can watch the ground feeders and the aerial feeders.

2 No bird feeder? Slather some peanut butter on a stale bagel and hang it by a string in full view. Replace daily until the birds get the message out that there are good "eats" at your house.

3 Describe a bird that comes to your feeder in great detail right down to the color feathers on the tips of its wings.

4 Ask a grown-up to help you identify the bird in a children's bird identification book (a librarian can help you).

MORE FUN!

♥ Create a cut-paper bird mosaic. Tear lots of tiny pieces of colorful tissue paper. On a large piece of paper draw a basic bird body; then glue paper bits all over it. Oh, a beautiful bird to hang in your room!

♥ Play bird match. Cut out bird photos from old magazines. One person describes a bird and the other picks it out from all the pictures.

♥ Do a bird count. Each day, at about the same time, count how many birds are at your feeder.

STAR PICTURES

Look in the sky
    late in the night,
Oh, twinkling stars
    shining so bright.

What is your story
    told through the ages?
Searching for meaning
    heard from the sages.

LITTLE DIPPER

POLARIS

Upon first glance, stars appear to be in complete disarray in the sky. Take a closer look and you will begin to see individual stars and maybe even shapes of animals, objects, and people outlined by the stars.

1 Look up at the stars. Think about how it is that people the world over have always shared the sky because it doesn't belong to anyone or any country.

2 Now, look again more closely. Face north; you will see a very bright star in the sky, called the North Star, or Polaris. It can be seen all year long in exactly the same place.

The best time to go stargazing is when the sky is clear of clouds and the moon is just a small crescent. Bright moonlight makes it more difficult to see the stars.

MORE FUN!

❤ Do you see any shapes in the sky? What do the stars look like to you? A clown face or a small dog? Draw them by connecting the stars (like dots) and give them a name. Then tell a story about how your star picture ended up in the night sky.

❤ Look carefully in the summer sky for shooting stars — stars that seem to shoot across the sky. Make a wish when you see one!

A PERFECT PACKAGE

Plant a seed in the ground,
A perfect package you have found!
Water it and give it care
A sprout will soon be growing there.

HERE'S WHAT YOU NEED

Bean seeds

Potting soil

Peat pots

HERE'S WHAT YOU DO

1 Push two seeds about one-half inch (1 cm) deep into each pot. Fill with soil and water lightly.

2 Set in sunlight or under a grow light.

3 Water regularly but do not soak seeds (or they will rot).

4 Every few days, cut open one seed from each pot (with a grown-up's help), and you will see how a seed develops into a plant. Isn't that a perfect package?

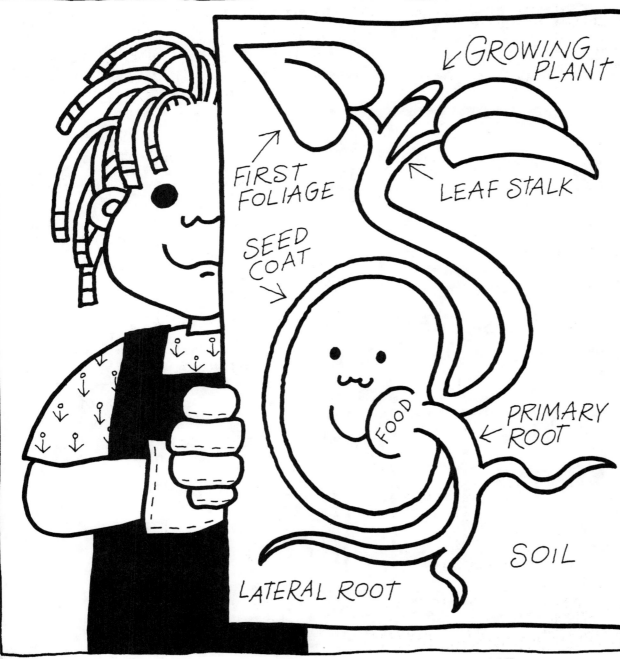

GROWING PLANT

FIRST FOLIAGE

LEAF STALK

SEED COAT

FOOD

PRIMARY ROOT

SOIL

LATERAL ROOT

MORE FUN!

♥ Transplant your seedlings outdoors when the ground is warm. Soon garden-fresh beans will be yours to eat — right off the vine!

EXPAND YOUR WORLD

A seed is a perfect package. It contains all the food and nourishment that it needs to begin life. All it needs is soil (or a growing medium), water, and warmth to grow — and that is what you can provide.

HELLO, SELF!

Hello, eyes, big and brown
Hello, mouth, why the frown?

Hello, hair, shiny and bright
Hello, me, why I'm just right!

We notice lots of things about other people right down to their fun freckles, curly hair, and bright, white teeth. But, what about you? After all, when was the last time you really studied those elbows of yours?

HERE'S WHAT YOU NEED

Large piece of butcher paper

Marker

Full-length mirror (or instant-develop camera)

HERE'S WHAT YOU DO

1 Stand in the mirror and look at your wonderful self — from head to toe. Pretty nice, huh!

2 Lie down on the paper and ask a partner to outline your body. You can even lie down in a pose with an arm bent.

3 Now you add the details that make you, you! Long hair or short? Big hands or little? Freckles on your nose or a dimple in your chin? Do you have a bruise on your knee from falling off your bike? Make sure to draw it. After all, it is a part of you.

MY PORTRAIT

MORE FUN!

♥ Color in your self-portrait using markers. Draw your portrait in your favorite clothes and baseball cap.

♥ Add other objects to your self-portrait, like a soccer ball or ballet slippers or a book — whatever describes you.

♥ Show your portrait to some friends and see if they can guess who it is.

♥ Make a portrait of your pet.

EXPAND YOUR WORLD

Start a scrapbook of your favorite things. Save a bookmark that you got at the bookstore or the tickets from the baseball game. Cut out pictures of things you like to do and to eat. Add some photos of special days and people. Paste them all in a scrapbook made of construction paper and tied together with yarn.

MY SCRAP- BOOK

TOUCH WILL TELL

Too hot or too cold, soft and furry or scratchy like sandpaper — our sense of touch tells us a lot about the world around us.

MITTEN PLAY

*Bet you can't guess
What's in your hand,
With mittens on
Can't feel the sand.*

We all wear mittens to keep our hands warm on a cold day. Have you ever worn mittens to see how important your sense of touch is? Probably not, but put them on anyway and have some fun.

1 Put a mitten on one hand and keep the other hand bare; then close your eyes.

2 Ask a partner to place different things in your mitten hand.

3 Can you guess what is in your hand with a mitten on? Then, move the object to your bare hand.

4 What does this mitten experiment tell you about your sense of touch?

EXPAND YOUR WORLD

Mittens are used to protect your hands from the cold. There are many kinds of gloves used to protect your hands from other things like heat or dirt. How many special hand-protecting gloves can you name?

BASEBALL GLOVE

LEATHER WORKING GLOVES

RUBBER GLOVES

GARDENING GLOVES

MORE FUN!

♥ What's one thing we all do with mittens? Lose one! Listen to *The Mitten* by Jan Brett for a wonderful tale of a lost mitten.

♥ Which do you like better — mittens or gloves? Talk about your preferences at dinner tonight. Are there more mitten fans or glove fans?

♥ See how many contraptions you and your friends can dream up to keep track of your mittens. Would magnets work?

TEXTURE TUNE-UP

"Hard as a rock,"
I heard her say,
About some bread
Baked yesterday!

Texture refers to how something feels. There are many words to describe exactly how something feels. Here's a fun way to build a texture word collection.

HERE'S WHAT YOU NEED

Sandpaper

Lotion

Stone

Cotton

HERE'S WHAT YOU DO

1 Touch each of the four objects listed on page 110, and match one of these descriptive words with each one:

soft, hard, smooth, rough

2 What else is rough like sandpaper?

3 What else is smooth like lotion?

4 Can you name something soft like cotton?

5 What can you think of that is hard like a rock?

THIS IS SMOOTH AS SILK

THIS IS ROUGH SANDPAPER

♥ Here are some more words that describe texture: **furry, prickly, bumpy, leathery, slippery, silky.** Can you name something that these words describe?

♥ Make up some texture tongue twisters. "The silly silky socks slid somewhere." How fast can you say them?

♥ Create a word. That's right, make up your own words to describe how something feels like "smoozy mud puddles."

BAREFOOT BONANZA

Step right up
Feet so bare;
Touch will tell
What is there!

What fun to go barefoot! As you skip along, your feet tell you about textures and temperatures. That's right, not only do your hands tell you a lot, but your feet "talk," too!

Before you walk barefoot, make sure there is no glass or sharp objects around (or too much dirt). Take a barefoot walk on:

- carpet
- tile floor
- grass
- sand
- cement
- mud
- a puddle

Can you describe how each surface feels to your feet? Here are some words you might use: **ticklish, gritty, cool, fuzzy, rough**.

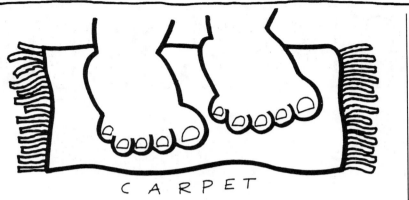

C A R P E T

G R A S S

M U D

MORE FUN!

❤ What if your feet really could speak? Make up a funny story about walking, talking feet.

❤ Mud puddles and bare feet! They're a perfect combination. Ask a grown-up if you can put on some old clothes and play in some mud puddles.

❤ Of course, animals are always walking barefoot. Look outdoors for some animal tracks. Decide how big the animal is and where it was going from studying its tracks.

❤ Make barefoot prints on the sidewalk. Wet your feet in some water and then make tracks.

BEACH TEXTURES

Sand tickles your toes,
Crabs nibble your feet;
A day at the beach
Simply cannot be beat.

A day at the beach could be called "Touch Awareness Day" because there are so many different textures and temperatures to feel and experience.

So while you are looking at hermit crabs and building sandcastles, take a beach walk and let your eyes, ears, nose, mouth — and hands and feet, too — get in on the fun!

1 Set a goal for the number of touch experiences you are going to "collect." Five, seven, or even ten?

2 Walk along and count the number of different textures and temperatures you come upon. Look for:

slimy seaweed

rippled scallop shells

smooth inner shells

porous coral pieces

brittle crab shells

coarse sand

powdery soft sand

rough barnacles

cold water

foamy waves

hot sand

oozing mud

prickly sunburn

MORE FUN!

♥ Collect some of your textured beach finds and bring them home to make a textured collage.

♥ Take a similar walk with a grown-up along the shore of a pond or lake. What kinds of different textures do you find? Are some textures the same?

♥ In the fall, take a Texture Forest Walk with a grown-up to see how many different textures you can discover.

♥ Collect sand in little baggies from different beaches. Then, compare how they feel and put them in order from most coarse to smoothest.

MY LEAF COLLAGE

EXPAND YOUR WORLD

When you visit a beach, don't forget to also collect litter. Bring along a brown paper bag to pick up litter like bottles, cans, and plastic rings. Pitching in is fun and important, too!

TOUCH HUNT

Where's something soft? Where's something smooth? Here's something furry — But it won't move!

There are so many different things to learn simply by touching. Here's a game that will test your touch-hunting skills. All you need is a partner — or you can play with a whole lot of people, too!

1 One person calls out a texture (say, sticky).

2 Everyone else finds something that is sticky (like a lollipop or jam jar) and brings it to the caller.

3 Continue calling and hunting. Then, switch callers.

STICKY STUFF!

❤ Take the Touch Hunt Challenge! Call out a texture **and** a shape (hard and round).

❤ Turn this game into a Touch Scavenger Hunt. List different textures on your hunt guide and then set out to collect the items in a bag.

❤ Find some things that are difficult to describe in one word, like a bean bag. Ask your friends or family what words they would choose to describe how these items feel.

HUNT LIST

BEYOND WORDS

There are so many ways to greet people when you first see them. You can say "Hi," "Hello," "How's it going?" "Good Morning" — and that's just in the spoken English language! But there are also other ways to let people know what you are thinking and how you are feeling — without ever speaking a word.

BODY LANGUAGE

A gesture,
A shrug,
A nod, or
A hug.

Sometimes our bodies — the way we hold our hands, the expression on our faces, the way we position our heads — tell people a lot about how we are feeling about ourselves and about them.

Without speaking, how would you communicate each of the following (there are lots of ways to do these):

Say "Hi"

Respond to someone you are introduced to

Say "Bye"

Show you are surprised

Show you are sad or happy

Let someone know you are glad to see them

Show that something tastes good or bad

Show someone you are angry

Show that you love someone

Show that you are feeling shy

Invite someone to sit on the sofa beside you

Signal someone to stop

Signal someone to move forward

Signal someone to be very quiet.

❤ Role play with a partner, and see how this body language makes your partner feel. Then, switch places.

Hold your arms straight out, with your hands palms out.

Lift your arms at your side, slightly curved inward, hands curved inward, too.

Sit with your arms folded in front of you.

Look at someone who is speaking to you.

Hold your head up high.

Stand up straight or stand slouching.

❤ Do you like to play sports? Ask a sports fan to show you the hand signals umpires use in sports to call a play.

❤ Learn to say hello in some other languages such as Spanish, French, German, Hebrew, Russian, or Italian.

EXPAND YOUR WORLD

American Sign Language (ASL) is one method that hearing-impaired people use to communicate. It is a very beautiful, expressive language. There are hand signs for each letter of the alphabet and there are also signs for words and phrases that are used frequently. Here is how to sign "I love you" in ASL.

TIME OUT

When you are sad and feeling blue,
Here is something you can do.
Instead of moping in a pout,
Treat yourself to a "time out."

Sometimes, when you are feeling sad, out of sorts, or getting into arguments with everyone around you, it is time to stop and treat yourself to a "time out."

1 Bring a few things that make you happy (like a favorite stuffed animal or book) to a quiet place where you can sit.

2 Spend this time alone, thinking about things that make you happy. Sometimes, just listening to your favorite song or looking at a funny picture will lift your spirits.

3 Remember to take as much time as you need. You may cheer up very quickly, or it may take a little time to feel better.

MORE FUN!

♥ Cheer up someone else . . . and you're sure to feel better, too. Make a Happy Days card or surprise someone with homemade brownies. Or, set aside a shared time out, just listening and talking to one other person. That way you both will feel better!

♥ Pick some fresh wild-flowers or dried weeds to put in your room.

♥ Start a scrapbook to help you remember fun times you've had. Put drawings, photographs, and funny jokes in your scrapbook. When you are sad, you can tickle your memories with your scrapbook.

RAINBOW WONDERS

'Tis said the rainbow will lead to gold,
  (Or at least that's how the story's told.)
I saw a rainbow of orange, blue, and red,
  But I could not see where the rainbow led.

A rainbow is a total sensory experience — the earth smells fresh after the rain, the birds are chirping, the grass feels wet on your bare feet — and then you look up to see a most amazing, colorful arc in the sky. What a beautiful surprise!

1 Perfect rainbow-hunting conditions: The rain has just stopped, there is still a fine mist in the air, and the sun is suddenly shining brightly (even as the last drops are still falling).

2 If possible, stand somewhere that gives you the greatest view of the open sky.

3 Look for a rainbow of color and let your eyes follow its arc as far as you can see.

EXPAND YOUR WORLD

The seven colors of the rainbow are red, orange, yellow, green, blue, indigo (a shade of bright blue), and violet (a purple-blue color). Get out your crayons and watercolors to paint a rainbow you can keep.

RED
ORANGE
YELLOW
GREEN
BLUE
INDIGO
VIOLET

MY RAINBOW

MORE FUN!

❤ Make your own outdoor mini-rainbows. Stand outside with your back to the sun. Hold a water hose in front of you and place your thumb over the opening to make a fine spray.

❤ Prisms make great rainbows. Start a prism collection in your room and hang each one with fishing line in a sunny window.

❤ Make a rainbow gelatin parfait using a sundae glass and different-flavored gelatins. This is fun to look at, and even more fun to eat!

A WALK IN THE DARK

*Walk in the dark
Without a glow,
Sounds and textures
You'll come to know.*

Some of us develop such a strong sense of sight that we forget to use all our other senses to their full potential. Here is something to do with a grown-up that will help you realize just how much you can do with your other senses.

1 With your grown-up partner, find a very safe space to wander around. Be sure there are no stairs, no water, nothing breakable like a flower vase, and nothing hot to bump into like a wood stove.

2 Close the window shades and close your eyes. No talking.

3 Walking very slowly, move your outstretched arms and try to cross the room. Do you hear the cat purring on the floor? That's a hearing signal to walk around it.

4 Did your hand or leg brush up against some furniture? Using your touch signal, walk around it.

5 Do you smell your brother's bubble gum? Then, use your smell signal to walk around him.

EXPAND YOUR WORLD

A Seeing Eye Dog is a specially trained dog that helps a sight-impaired person. These dogs have a very important job to do. When you see one (you will recognize it by the handle-harness it wears), don't pet the dog or call to it. Remember, it is a dog at work.

MORE FUN!

♥ Open your eyes. What couldn't you possibly know without your sense of sight?

♥ Close your eyes and have your partner place different objects in your hand. Try to guess what they are by using your senses of touch and smell.

♥ Some sight-impaired people move a white-tipped cane in front of them. How do you think this might help?

ANIMAL CHARADES

What is that person trying to be?
Guessing's the goal for you and for me.
One plays the actor, sort of a mime,
Call out your guesses one at a time.

Play Animal Charades with two or more people. One person acts out an animal's movements and appearance, trying to communicate without actually saying anything. The goal here is to listen with your eyes, not your ears. How would you:

swing like a monkey,

show an elephant's trunk,

stretch like a giraffe,

walk like a penguin,

strut like a turkey,

sniff like a bunny?

If you visit a **zoo**, you will see different kinds of animals. If you visit an **aquarium**, you will see many kinds of sea life. Some people don't think there should be zoos and aquariums because the animals are taken away from their natural **habitats** (the places where they would live naturally). What do you think?

MORE FUN!

♥ Cut out pictures of animals from old magazines. Put them in a bag. Each player secretly draws a picture and acts out the animal for the others to guess.

♥ Can you arrange a trip to a zoo or a pet store? It is great fun. Notice how each animal behaves and moves. Then, go home and play Animal Charades.

♥ Play "If I Were" using animal names. "If I were a puppy, I would . . ."

SHAPE SIGNS

*Eight-sided and red —
A good sign to know,
So, what does it mean?
Shout, "When NOT to go!"*

Signs give us messages by their shapes and colors. Other messages come from lights and symbols (pictures). Many of them help keep us safe; others give us helpful information — no matter what language we speak.

1 Ask a grown-up to take you for a ride. Take a pad and paper to draw all the signs that you see without words. Then, talk about what each sign means. Did you see a railroad crossing sign or a curve-in-the-road sign?

2 Did you see a great big ice-cream cone next to a restaurant? What does that sign tell you?

3 What are the signs that tell people "No Smoking"?

♥ Make some signs using shapes and symbols for your house or classroom. Create signs saying "exit," "slippery floor," "beware of dog," "no smoking," "turn here."

♥ Talk about the different kinds of lights and sirens that you see and hear. You know what a red light and a green light mean, but do you know what a flashing blue light on a car means?

STOP, LOOK & LISTEN!

*B*efore you start to cross the street,
Or take a kettle off the heat,
On the road or in the kitchen,
Don't forget: Stop, Look and Listen!

Some rules make such good sense that we all need to follow them no matter how old or young we are. Stop, Look and Listen is one of those rules to always follow. You'll be using your observation skills to keep you safe.

1. Review the rules for crossing the street. Then, play "Practice Walk" with a grown-up.

2. One person is the teller and the other is the (pretend) walker.

3. The teller makes up a pretend situation, something like this: "You are playing outside when your ball rolls into the street." The walker shouts, " Stop, Look and Listen" and tells why.

4. Then, switch roles.

Stop, Look, and Listen is the golden rule for crossing the street. There are no exceptions. Always:

STOP at the cross-walk while you are still standing on the curb;

LOOK both ways to make sure no cars are coming;

LISTEN for the sounds of cars, trains, or bikers coming.

Then, if all is clear, holding a grown-up's hand, look again, and cross carefully.

REMEMBER:
STOP,
LOOK &
LISTEN!

MORE FUN!

❤ In what other situations is it especially important to stop, look and listen? What about in the kitchen?

❤ Why shouldn't you run across the street?

❤ Say "Good Morning" to your school crossing guard or bus driver every day.

❤ Why do you think this important rule has the "Listen" part in it?

INDEX TO ACTIVITIES